EXTRA! EXTRA!

Advanced Reading & Writing Activities for Language Arts

Terri L. Crowder

ISBN 1-59363-024-7

Prufrock Press, Inc.
P.O. Box 8813
Waco, Texas 76714-8813
(800) 998-2208
Fax (800) 240-0333
http://www.prufrock.com

Table of Contents

Introduction to Teachers and Parents

This book is designed for K–2 advanced learners in the area of language arts. Its content is designed to encourage the student to think about language and strengthen his or her ability to communicate an idea or thought. Activities demonstrate the importance of reading and writing well. They also point to the large part that language plays in our everyday life through a number of venues.

Some very young students are advanced in one area such as reading, but their writing ability may be at or only slightly above grade level. This book contains several activities that allow students the option of writing, illustrating, or acting out their activity. Some students may enjoy doing all three. The parent or teacher is free to tailor the activities to meet the student's needs and abilities since each activity is self-contained. In other words, a student is not required to complete the first activity before moving to the second and third and so on.

There is a "Read Me First" portion preceding each section of activities. "Read Me First" provides background information on the theme of that section of activities and some preliminary instructions. This portion may be read aloud to the student if needed. At the end of each activity, students can complete a "What Have I Learned?" questionnaire that will serve as a review of the activity, as well as provide an additional opportunity for expressing themselves and strengthening their language and writing skills. *There are no right or wrong answers in regard to content, but the teacher or parent may choose to take advantage of one or more activities to instruct in the correct use of grammar, capitalization, or punctuation.*

The "Supplies Needed for Activity" heading at the start of each activity will list any supplies needed/desired for each individual activity. Please note: The items are considered to be general classroom supplies to which the student will probably already have access, e.g., scissors, glue, and crayons.

Goals of the Activity Book

1. Provide young, advanced learners with age appropriate activities and material.

2. Present activities for various learning styles (e.g., visual or hands-on).

3. Provide activities for use in a public or home education setting for a single student or group of students.

Skills Addressed by Activities

Students will complete activities designed to develop skills in alignment with nationally accepted curriculum skills and content requirements defined by the Texas Education Agency (http://www.tea.state.tx.us/teks) for grade levels 2–5. Some of the skills listed include a blend of grade levels that may be represented by an advanced learner in grades K-2.

Continued on the next page …

Reading

- Read and comprehend a variety of second through fifth grade level texts

- Demonstrate characteristics of fluent and effective reading

- Read for enjoyment, to solve problems, to gather information, and to extend vocabulary

- Retell or act out important events in a story

- Use knowledge of syntax (word order) and semantics (word meaning) to identify unfamiliar words

- Support responses to readings by referring to relevant aspects of the text and their own experiences

Writing

- Write messages using their knowledge of letters and sounds

- Record or dictate ideas, stories

- Gain increasing control of penmanship and punctuation

- Compose questions, ideas, and stories

- Write original texts for varied purposes, such as composing lists, letters, stories and poems, as well as make precise word choices and create vivid images that may include dialogue and figurative language

- Engage in the writing process by generating ideas before writing and developing and polishing drafts

- Compose complete sentences in written texts and use appropriate end punctuation

- Evaluate written compositions using assigned and established criteria

- Write to express discover, record, develop, reflect on ideas and problem solve, as well as to persuade, argue and request

- Compose journals, letters, reviews, poems, narratives, and instructions

Listening/Speaking

- Present dramatic interpretations of experiences, stories, poems and plays

- Listen responsively to stories and other texts read aloud

- Gain increasing control of grammar, such as subject-verb agreement, complete sentences and correct tense usage

- Identify how language, such as labels and sayings, reflects regions and cultures

Viewing/Representing

- Produce visual images, messages and meanings that communicate effectively

- Produce class newspapers, multimedia reports and/or short films

Newspaper Activities Read Me First!

Newspapers are a great way to give or receive information. They tell us about weather, sports, and events in our community. They entertain us with comic strips and challenge us with crossword puzzles. We can also read about special people and amazing stories.

Here is an opportunity for you to publish your own newspaper or a single newspaper article. You will be completing one or more of the following activities. *You* can decide what to write and/or illustrate:

1. **Weather forecast**

2. **Sports event**

3. **Comic strip**

4. **Crossword puzzle**

5. **Article about a special event or person**

6. **Letter to the newspaper editor**

When a reporter begins writng, he or she will usually include specific information. The person will ask the following questions about what has been written:

Who? What? When? Where? Why? How?

If you choose to describe an event or person, ask yourself the five questions about what you've written. This will help you decide if your article is complete or if it needs more information.

Use your imagination and have fun. You may be a published writer one day with an editor to please, but for the next few minutes you're in charge of what you write!

Weather Forecast

Supplies Needed For Activity:
pencil or pen

Have you ever watched the weather forecast on TV? Did you know that it is also found in the newspaper? When you want to go to the park or take a vacation you might be curious about the forecast. Now you get to be in charge! To make your own extended weather forecast, describe the weather for each school day on the lines provided. For example, Monday may be mostly sunny and Thursday may be rainy.

Monday: _____

Tuesday:_____

Wednesday: _____

Thursday: _____

Friday: _____

Weather Forecast

Supplies Needed For Activity:

pen or pencil, crayons

Look back at your written weather forecast. Next, draw your own pictures of the weather for each day in the boxes below. You may want your pictures to look like those at the bottom of the page.

Mon.	
Tues.	
Wed.	
Thurs.	
Fri.	

Sports Page

Supplies Needed For Activity:
pen or pencil

Do you have a favorite sport that you like to watch on TV? Do you play a sport? Which sport do you know a lot about? This is your chance to write your own article for the sports page! Remember to ask yourself the following questions before you start writing: Who? What? When? Where? Why? How?

Sports by: _____

_____

_____

_____

_____

_____

_____

_____

Comic Strip

Supplies Needed For Activity:
pen or pencil, crayons

Have you ever read the "funnies"? Do you have a favorite comic strip? Does it make you smile or laugh? Comics are usually light-hearted, and the "joke" is easily understood. Now you can create your own! Answering the following questions may help you get started. On the next page, you will draw the cartoon itself.

Who are your characters?

_____

Where are they?

_____

What are they doing?

_____

When did this happen?

_____

Why or **How** did this happen?

_____

Comic Strip

Once you have made plans for your comic strip, draw your cartoon in the spaces below. Did you know that some comics have bubbles that show what the characters are saying or thinking? That is called **dialogue** ("di-a-log"). Did you remember to include what the characters are saying to each other? You can color the pictures or leave them in black and white.

Crossword Puzzle

Supplies Needed For Activity:

pen or pencil, crayons

Do you like solving puzzles? Today you get to design your own! To begin, decide what the clues and answers will be and write them down. They can be about anything! You may want to include your favorite food, movie star, or even your favorite color.

Next, assign the answers a place on the puzzle. The answers should read up and down or left to right. Some of the answers will overlap. Be sure to include the clue number in the first letter of each word on the puzzle. You do not have to fill in every space with letters. When you are finished, color in the empty spaces that do not have letters in them. On the next page, there are clues and answers to help you get started. That page is where you will plan out your puzzle. It will also be your answer sheet for the real puzzle when you are finished.

Page 9 is a blank puzzle. Write your clues again at the bottom of that page, but leave the puzzle blank except for the clue numbers. Be careful to write the numbers in the correct boxes. You may also go ahead and color in the boxes that will not have letters in them. Take time to make sure that you color only the boxes that will not have answers in them by comparing the second page with the answer sheet.

Crossword Puzzle

(Planning/Answer Sheet)

[1.] L	U	N	[2.] C	H					
			A						
			M						
			E						
			L						

Across

1. A meal eaten in the middle of day

Down

2. Animal with a humped back

Crossword Puzzle

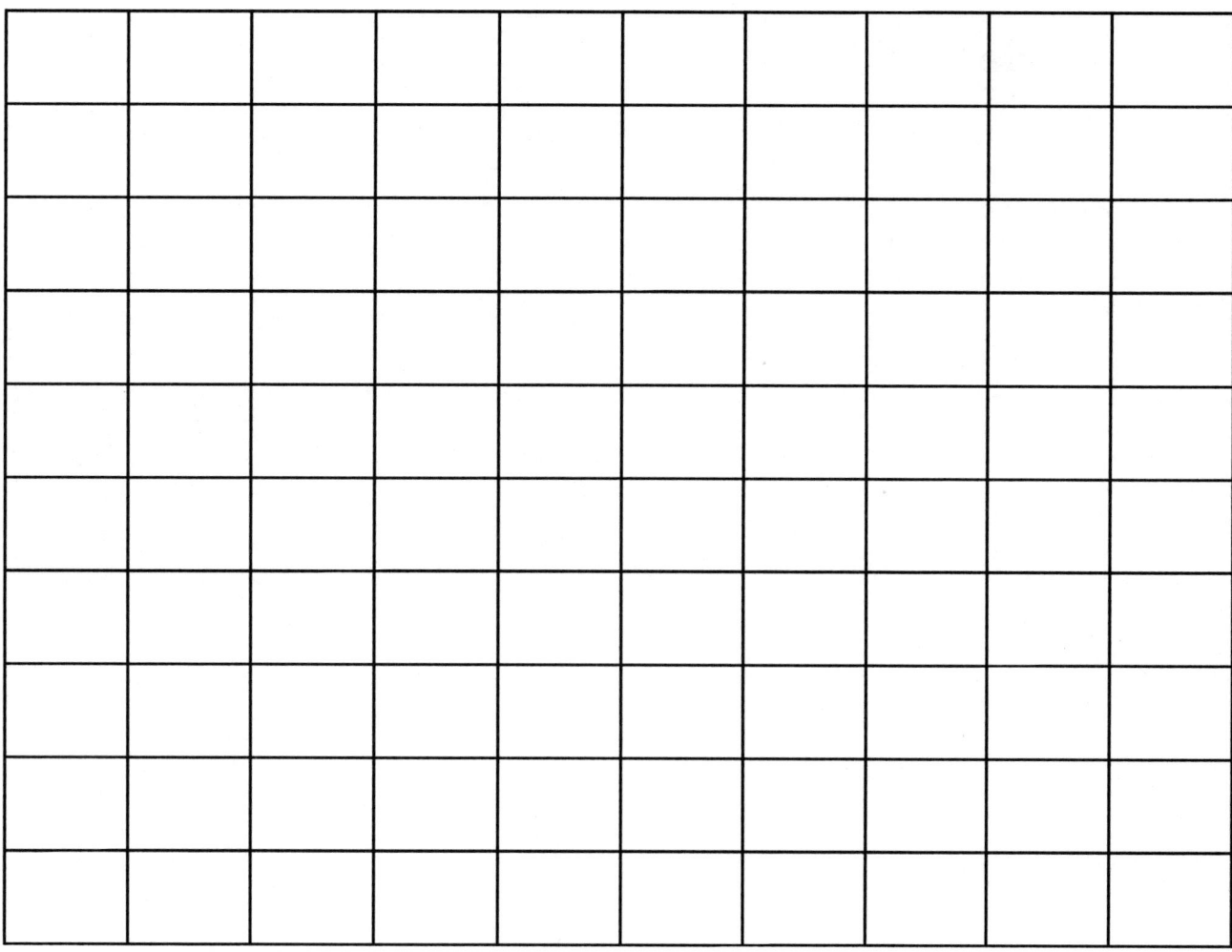

Across   **Down**

Special Events or People

Supplies Needed For Activity:
pen or pencil

Would you like to write a newspaper article about something happening in your school, neighborhood, or town? Would you like to write about a special person? This is the activity for you! Take a minute to think about what you want to write. Remember to ask yourself the following questions before you start writing: Who? What? When? Where? Why? How? Don't forget to give your article a title.

_____

By: _____

_____

_____

_____

_____

_____

_____

Letter to the Editor

Supplies Needed For Activity:
pen or pencil

When someone writes a letter to the editor of a newspaper, it may be about something:

1. Important to them
2. They want other people to know about
3. They have strong feelings or opinions about
4. They want to change

Answer the following questions. Then use the answers to write a letter to an imaginary editor.

What is important to you?

_____

Who would you like to tell?

_____

How do you feel about it?

_____

Where is it happening?

_____

Why do you think it should change?

_____

Letter to the Editor

Dear Editor:

_____

_____

_____

_____

_____

_____

_____

_____

_____

Sincerely,

_____

(Sign your name on this line)

Invent-A-Word Activities Read Me First!

Have you ever wondered where a word came from? Maybe it sounded strange to you or perhaps you thought it should be called something else. Many words have more than one meaning even when they are spelled the same. These words are called **homonyms.** Here are a few examples:

"Train" can mean to "teach or instruct." It can also be defined as a vehicle that carries passengers or cargo and moves on railroad tracks. A third definition refers to a long part of a dress or gown.

"Fan" can mean something used to cool the air or a person who is very enthusiastic about something or someone.

It can be very interesting to think about how one word has come to mean different things. At one time or another, someone used a word that had never been used before. Other people heard the new word, began to use it, and before long it was part of everyday conversation.

Wouldn't it be fun to know how a word and its meaning began? Here is your chance. Use your imagination and invent a word that has never been used before! Don't forget to share your new word with your friends. Use the word and see how quickly others start using it, too!

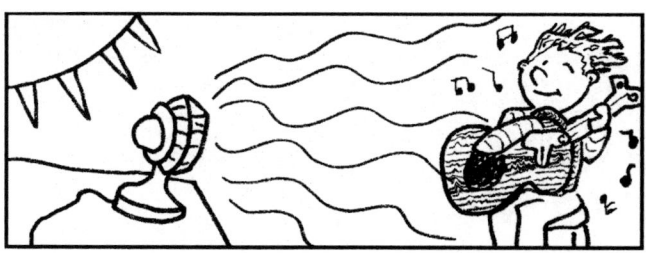

When we learn new words, we add to our vocabulary. The more words we have to express ourselves, the more successful we will be in communicating with others. The next few activities will help strengthen your vocabulary.

Choose one or more of the following:

1. **Invent a new word to begin your own dictionary.**

2. **Write a story about a new word.**

3. **Illustrate (draw a picture) a new word.**

4. **Write an original skit about a new word.**

Invent It

Supplies Needed For Activity:
pen or pencil

Now it's your turn to invent a word. If you are working alone, you may invent more than one word if time permits. If you are working with friends, put all the new words together in a booklet to form a dictionary.

Write your new word here:

_____

What does it mean?

_____

How will the word be used?

_____

Who will use the word the most?

_____

Use your new word in a sentence.

_____

_____

Tell A Story

Supplies Needed For Activity:
pen or pencil

Write a story about a new word you have invented. You can write about how it was first used or it can simply be a story in which the characters use the word. Be creative and make it fun! Remember to ask yourself: Who? What? When? Where? Why? How?

_____

_____

_____

_____

_____

_____

_____

_____

_____

_____

Illustrate It

Supplies Needed For Activity:

pen or pencil, crayons

Draw a picture that shows someone using a new word. Be sure to include lots of details so your picture tells a complete story. **Hint:** If you have already written a story about your invented word, you may refer to it so that your picture tells a complete story.

Write a Skit

Supplies Needed For Activity: pen or pencil, scissors, glue, or tape

This activity is a short play that you will write and then act out with finger puppets. The puppet patterns have been provided in the activity book for your skit. Draw your characters on these patterns. Since the puppets are used on your fingers, you may play the parts of all the characters yourself. If you are completing this activity with friends, you will want to make sure there are enough characters in the skit for each student to play at least one role.

You may write your skit about any topic that interests you. To begin, you will need to decide the following:

1. **What** your skit will be about and its title.

2. **Where** and **when** it will take place.

3. **Who** your characters will be and **how** they came to be at the place where your skit begins.

Be sure to have your characters use a new word that you have invented!

Write a Skit

Begin writing the skit by listing the name of the character that will speak first.

Next to the character's name, write what that person will say.

Write what the next character will say on a new line.

Continue with the other characters to tell your story until "The End."

_____

(Title of Skit)

Characters:_____

_____

Setting (When and where skit is taking place):

_____

Purpose (Message or lesson you want to share in the skit):

_____

_____

Name:_____ **Date:**_____

Write a Skit

_____

_____

_____

_____

_____

_____

_____

_____

_____

_____

_____

_____

_____

_____

Continue on another sheet of paper if you need to.

Write A Skit

Cut out the finger puppets. Use glue or tape to fasten the tabs together to form a loop that will fit your fingers. Decide which puppet will play which character and you're ready to start!

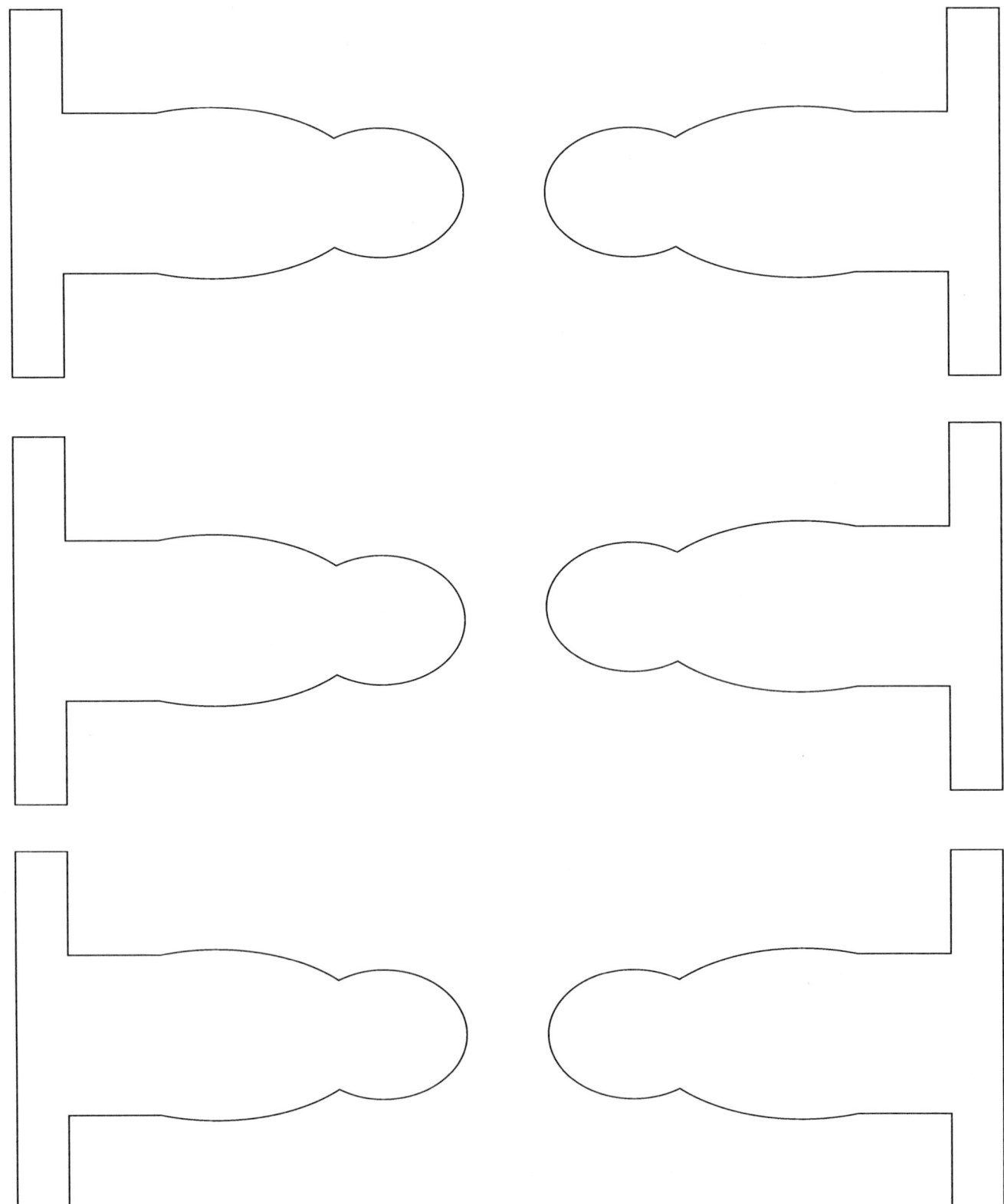

 Extra! Extra! ©2005 by Terri L. Crowder/ Illustrations ©2005 by Mike Eustis

The World Around Me—Read Me First!

A **neighborhood** is an area of the city or town in which we live. The homes next-door, across the street, or even a few blocks down the street can be considered part of our neighborhood.

There are many members of a **community**. A community is larger than a neighborhood. It may be your entire town, or one section of a very large city. It can include the mailman who delivers mail, the fire department who is always ready to help if we call, and the policemen who patrol the area to keep us safe. If you live in a very small town, your doctor's office, grocery store, and other places you visit often may also be close by. If you live in a large city, they may be quite a distance away.

The **state** you live in is a much larger area than a neighborhood or community. The state where you live is different from all of the others in many ways. Each state has its own unique name, capital city, size, and shape. There are both mountains and beaches in some states, and some states have neither. Even the kinds of animals and plant life can be very different from state to state.

Our country, the United States of America, which consists of 50 different states, is a country of diversity. "Diversity" means there many differences.

Continued on the next page …

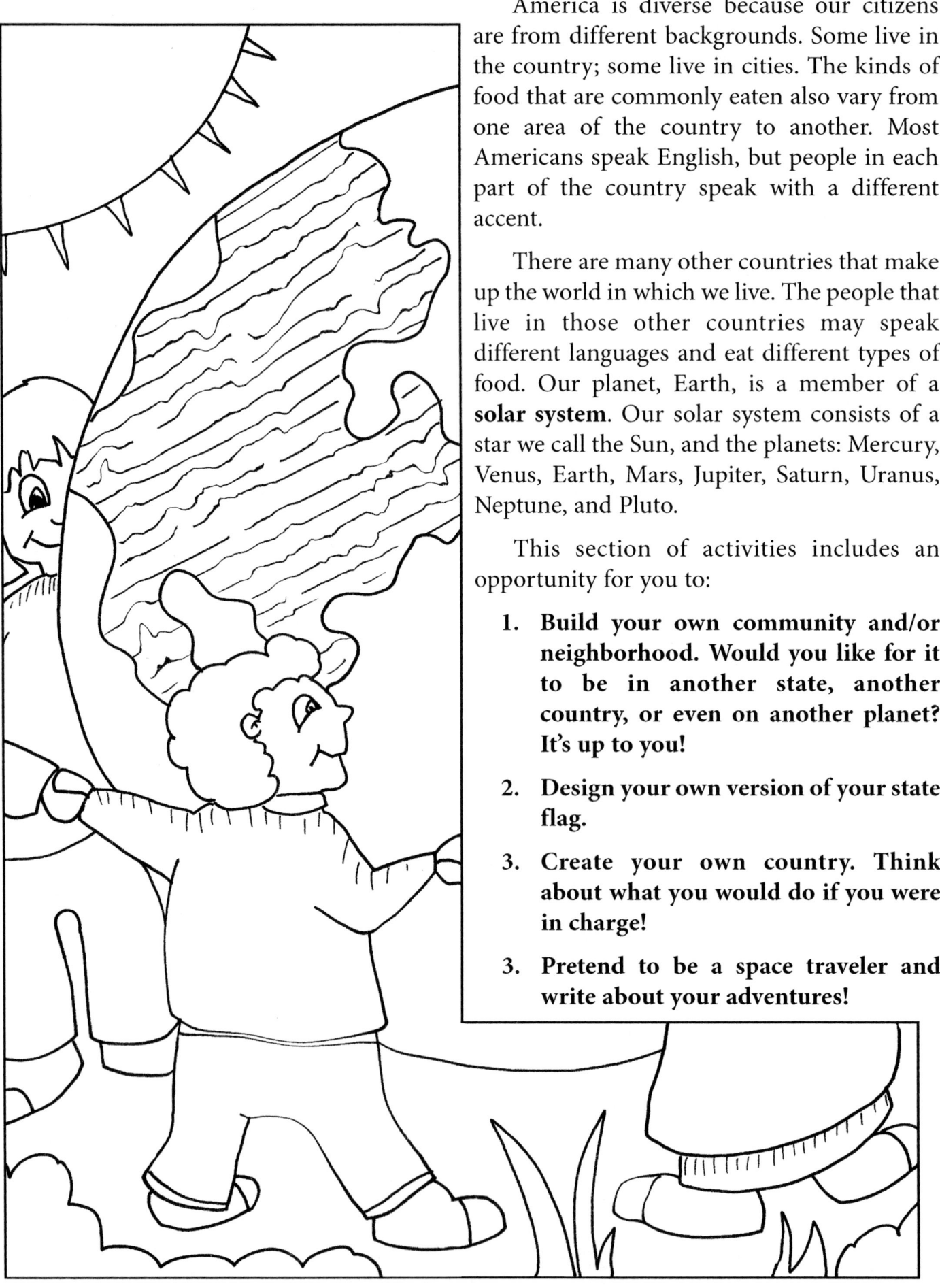

America is diverse because our citizens are from different backgrounds. Some live in the country; some live in cities. The kinds of food that are commonly eaten also vary from one area of the country to another. Most Americans speak English, but people in each part of the country speak with a different accent.

There are many other countries that make up the world in which we live. The people that live in those other countries may speak different languages and eat different types of food. Our planet, Earth, is a member of a **solar system**. Our solar system consists of a star we call the Sun, and the planets: Mercury, Venus, Earth, Mars, Jupiter, Saturn, Uranus, Neptune, and Pluto.

This section of activities includes an opportunity for you to:

1. **Build your own community and/or neighborhood. Would you like for it to be in another state, another country, or even on another planet? It's up to you!**

2. **Design your own version of your state flag.**

3. **Create your own country. Think about what you would do if you were in charge!**

3. **Pretend to be a space traveler and write about your adventures!**

Build a Community

Supplies Needed For Activity:

pen or pencil

Now it's time for you to create your own community or neighborhood. You may want it to be very much like the community in which you live. You may choose for it to be very different. It's up to you!

1. The name of my imaginary community is:

_____

2. The language that is spoken is:

_____

3. My community is located:

_____

4. The people who live there like to eat:

_____

5. The people who live here wear clothes that look like:

_____

Name:______________________________ **Date:**____________

Build a Community

Supplies Needed For Activity:
scissors, tape or glue, drawing paper, crayons

To begin building your community, color the building patterns. Use the blank pattern to make your own special building. Cut out the buildings. Fold and fasten the flaps with tape or glue so the buildings will stand to form a community. You decide if you would like to arrange it to look like the community in which you live or if you would prefer to create a unique neighborhood from your imagination.

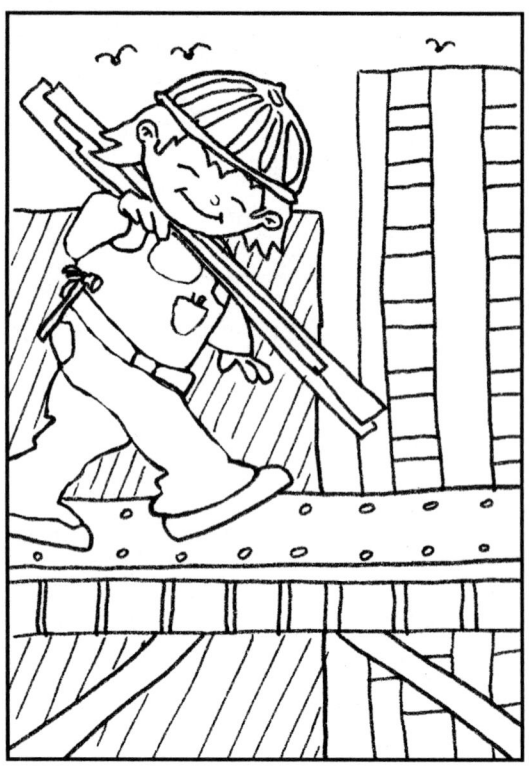

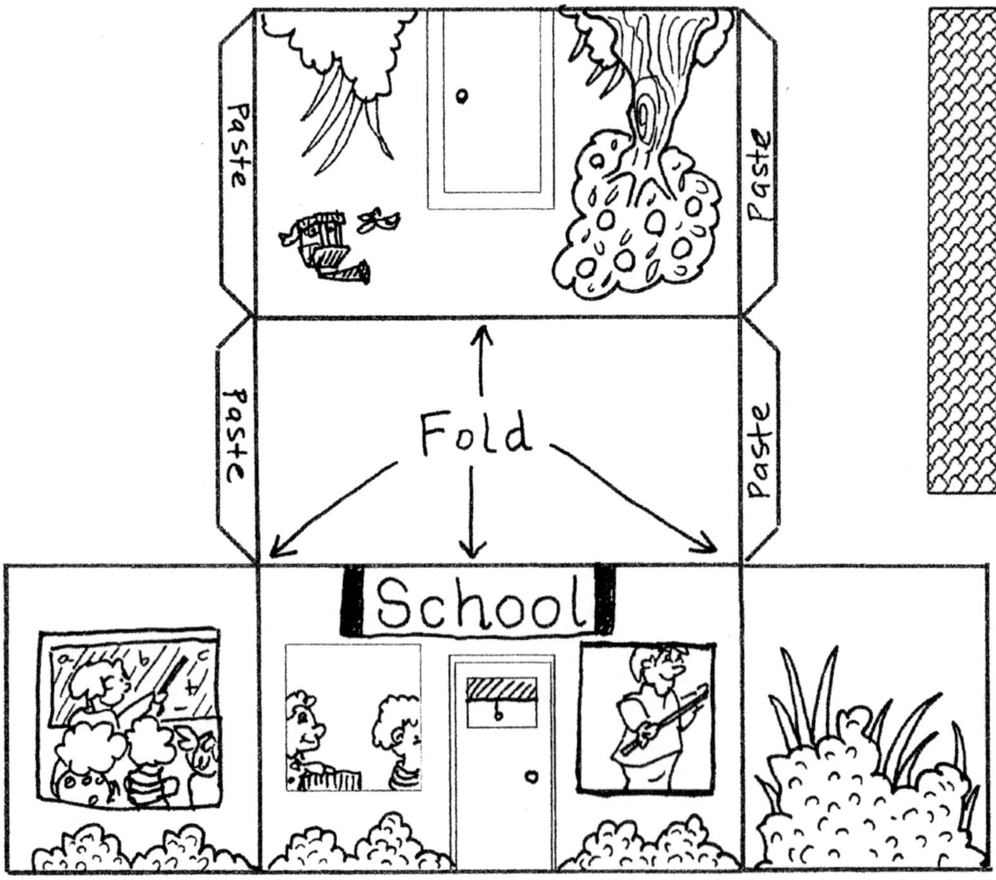
Paste
Paste
Paste
Paste
Fold
School

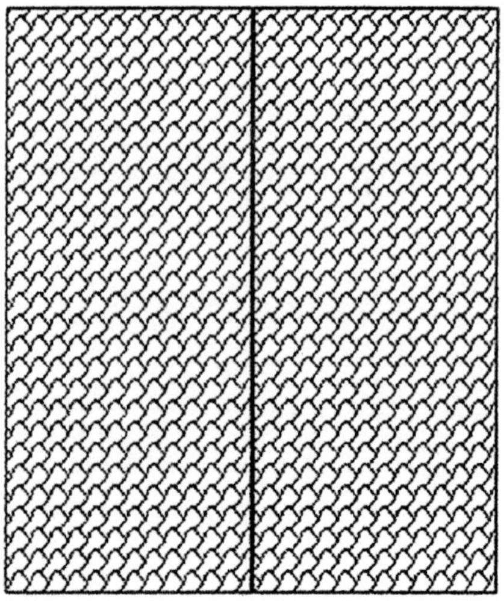

Build a Community

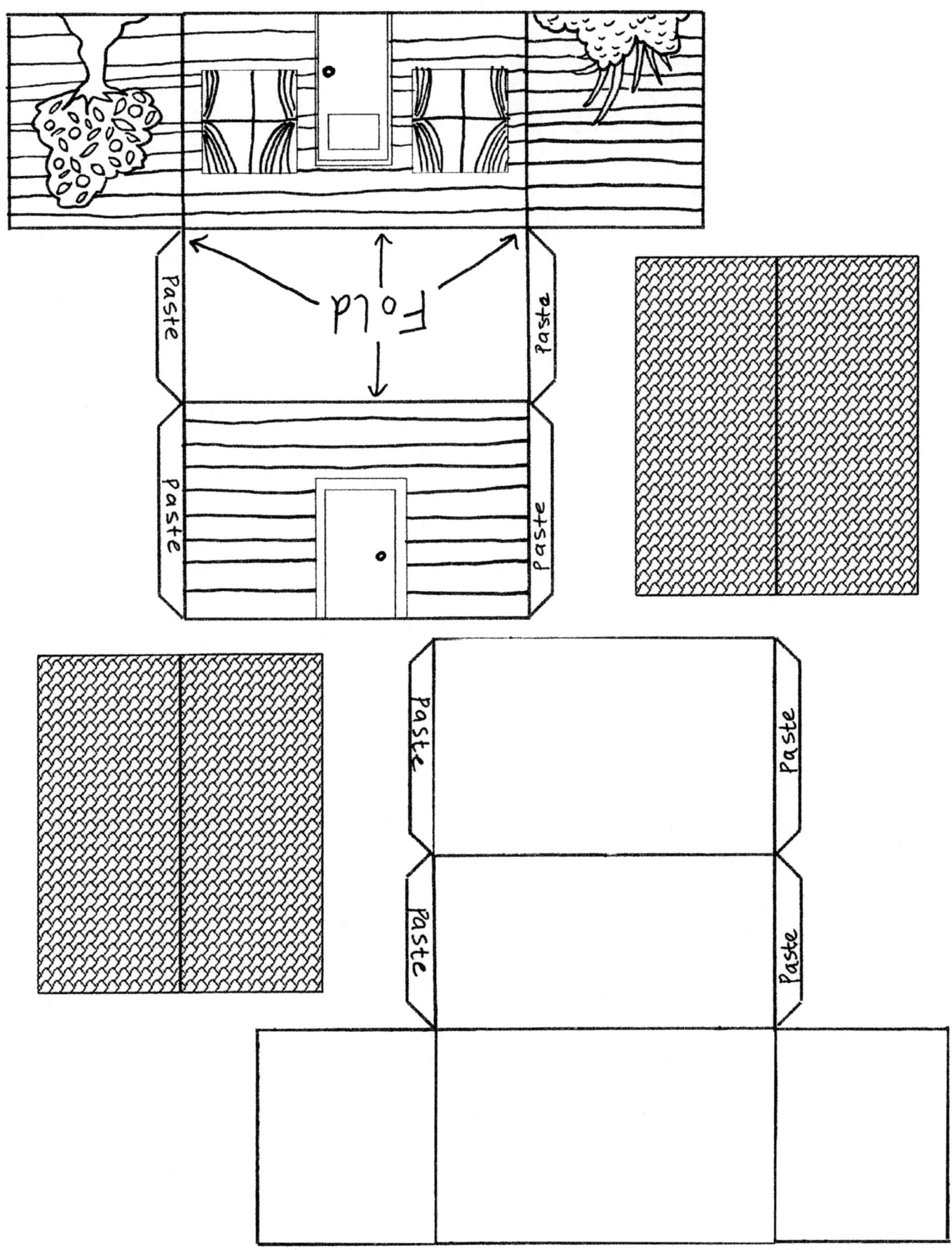

Build a Community

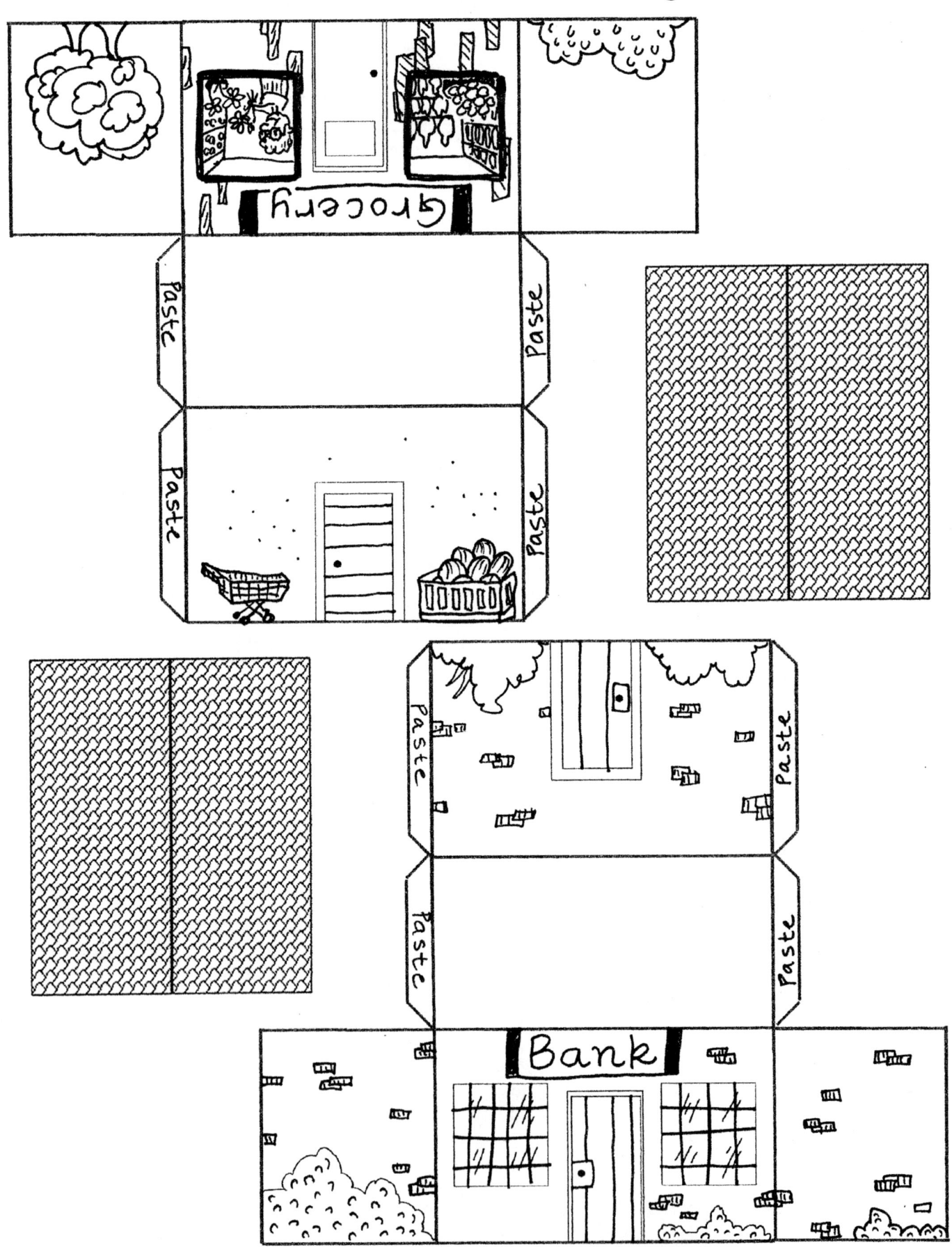

Extra! Extra! ©2005 by Terri L. Crowder/ Illustrations ©2005 by Mike Eustis

My State Flag

Supplies Needed For Activity:

pen or pencil, crayons, scissors, tape or glue, colored paper

Would you recognize your home state's flag? This activity allows you to design your own version of a state flag. It should include the state's name and pictures or words that symbolize what is special about your home state. For example, if you live in Florida, you might want to draw a picture of the sun, an orange blossom, or even an alligator. Create and color your flag in the space below.

Create a Country

Supplies Needed For Activity:

pen or pencil

There are many countries that make up the world in which we live. What if you were in charge of your own country? There are a number of important decisions that must be made! Complete the following statements about your new country:

1. The name of my imaginary country is:

_____

2. My country is located:

_____

3. The languages spoken are:

_____

4. My country's climate is:

_____

5. People would want to visit my country because:

_____

6. Three important rules or laws that people in my country should follow are:

_____

Name:_____ **Date:**_____

Create a Country

Supplies Needed For Activity:
pen or pencil, crayons

Draw a map of a new country that has never been discovered. Make sure to include things like oceans and rivers, mountains, deserts, forests, roads, or anything else that your country may have. Don't forget to put the capital city and other towns on the map.

Create a Country

Supplies Needed For Activity:

pen or pencil, crayons, scissors

Now you get to design a travel brochure for your new country. Brochures are usually very colorful and have a lot of exciting pictures. They also provide general information about the destination. Brochures usually answer questions that people may have such as:

- **Where is the destination located?**

- **What languages are spoken?**

- **What is the population?**

- **What is the weather like throughout the year?**

- **What kind of money is used?**

- **What is there to do while visiting the destination?**

Think about why people would want to visit your new country. Does it have mountains or beaches? Are there fun and exciting activities for people to do? Are there good restaurants where people can eat? What kind of hotels are in your country?

Decide how you will design your brochure. Will it have pictures of activities to do or places to visit in your country? Will you provide interesting facts about your country? It's up to you! Be sure to provide enough information to interest people who may want to come visit you in your new country. Brainstorm your ideas on a piece of paper and then use the next page to make the travel brochure for your country. When you have finished your brochure, cut it out, fold it on the dotted lines, and share it with your friends!

Extra! Extra!

Space Traveler

Supplies Needed For Activity:

pen or pencil

Our solar system consists of a star we call the Sun, and the planets Mercury, Venus, Earth, Mars, Jupiter, Saturn, Uranus, Neptune, and Pluto. To those of us on Earth, our planet appears to be large, but from outer space, astronauts often get the impression that the Earth is small!

Many people dream of traveling in space and viewing the wonders of the universe. Did you know we are **all** space travelers in a manner of speaking? Our spaceship is the Earth. It travels at about 67,000 miles an hour! It takes 365 days for the Earth to travel around the Sun and 24 hours for the Earth to rotate a complete revolution.

Are you ready to be a space traveler? Let's pretend you have just discovered a planet or world that no one has ever seen. Your spaceship has just landed.

Space Traveler

Describe your space adventure in as much detail as you can! Ask yourself these questions about the planet to help you begin. Where are the people and animals? What do they look like? Is the sky the same color as Earth's? What type of homes do they live in? What do they use for travel? What kind of plants and trees are there?

_____

_____

_____

_____

_____

_____

_____

_____

_____

Space Traveler

Supplies Needed For Activity:

pen or pencil, crayons

Draw a picture of what you see on the planet you've just discovered. Make sure you add lots of details to help your picture tell a complete story.

What Do You Think? Read Me First!

When someone asks us what we think about something, we enjoy sharing our opinion. Did you know how we think is just as important as what we think?

Solving problems is something we each do, but we don't always realize that's what we're doing. We make decisions every day about what to wear, when to eat, and what book to read. These are all are choices and decisions, but they are also the beginning of learning how to find solutions.

These activities will ask you to "solve" several different problems or situations. You will read a paragraph and then write or illustrate (you may do both if time permits) the solution. It is up to you. There may be more than one solution to each. What will your solution be?

Building With Boxes

Supplies Needed For Activity:

pen or pencil, crayons

Martin enjoys making things. He has a desk in his room where he keeps crayons, paper, scissors, glue, and tape. He really likes to build things using boxes. Today he has one large box, one small box, and two paper towel tubes. What can Martin make with these items? (Remember: he can also use the things he has in his desk.)

Describe what you would like Martin to build in words and/or draw a picture of his finished project.

Choosing Chairs

Supplies Needed For Activity:
pen or pencil, crayons

Logan and his parents eat dinner together every night at the table in their dining room. The chairs that Logan and his parents use are identical, and they each sit in the same place at each meal. The fourth chair doesn't match the other three. One evening before dinner Logan decides that he would like to sit in the unmatched chair. The table has already been set for dinner. Can he sit in the unmatched chair and not have to reset the table? How? Write or draw your answer.

Gardening Gloves

Supplies Needed For Activity:
pen or pencil, crayons

Katie likes to work in the vegetable garden with her grandmother. They go to the garden early each morning before school. Sometimes they pull weeds or till the ground with the garden hoe. One morning Grandmother asked Katie to bring her a pair of gloves. Katie tried very hard to find them because Katie knew Grandmother wanted the gloves to protect her hands. She couldn't find them, so she brought her grandmother something to use instead of gloves. What could be used that might protect Grandmother's hands? Draw or write your answer.

Name:_____ **Date:**_____

Trash or Treasure

Supplies Needed For Activity:
pen or pencil

When we recycle, we waste less. Many times we throw away items that could be used again. Look at the list below. Pick at least five things that have been thrown away that can be used again. On the line next to the item, write another use for the items.

Cereal Box _____

Coffee Can _____

Laundry Detergent Bottle _____

Popsicle Sticks _____

Comic Strips_____

Paper Towel/Toilet Paper Tubes_____

Kleenex Box _____

Milk Carton _____

Egg Carton _____

Whipped Topping Bowl _____

Baby Food Jar _____

Diaper Wipes Container_____

Disposable Cups_____

Name:_____ **Date:**_____

Worksheet
What Have I Learned?

What I enjoyed the most about this activity is:

_____

_____

If I were going to tell a friend about this activity, I would say:

_____

_____

One thing I learned from this activity is:

_____

_____

If I could start this activity again, I would change:

_____

_____

Did I do my best work on this activity? Why or why not?

_____

_____

ACTIVITIES FOR ADVANCED LEARNING SERIES

Camp Fraction
Solving Exciting Word Problems Using Fractions
Set around a trip to summer camp, students work with fractions in a problem-solving format, while learning a little history, trivia, and fun facts about a number of different items.
Grades 4–6 $11.95

Creative Writing
Using Fairy Tales to Enrich Writing Skills
Use fairy tales to challenge and motivate your students. This activity book contains fun reading and writing activities that pique students' interest in creative writing.
Grades 4–8 $11.95

Extra! Extra!
Advanced Reading and Writing Activities for Language Arts
The book includes standards-based independent language arts activities for students in grades K–2 such as developing a newspaper and inventing new words.
Grades K-2 $11.95

Math Problem Solvers
Using Word Problems to Enhance Mathematical Problem Solving Skills
The standards-based problem solving strategies addressed in this book include drawing a picture, looking for a pattern, guessing and checking, acting it out, making a table or list, and working backwards.
Grades 2–3 $11.95

Puzzled by Math!
Using Puzzles to Teach Math Skills
Puzzled by Math! offers a collection of mathematical equations, knowledge, and skills in puzzle form. Standards-based content addresses addition, subtraction, multiplication, division, fractions, decimals, and algebra. Thirty-five exciting and challenging puzzles are included, as well as suggestions for using the material for a classroom learning center.
Grades 3–7 $11.95

Survival on the Reef
Exploring Amazing Animals and the Ways They Adapt to Their Environment
This challenging activity book addresses many essential skills and knowledge contained in the National Science Teachers Association standards using activities focused on the exciting environment of a coral reef, its inhabitants, and the ways these inhabitants have adapted to their world.
Grades 2–3 $11.95

Writing Stretchers
15 Minute Activities to Enrich Writing Skills
Standards-based activities address the areas of reading, writing, vocabulary, content literacy, creativity, and thinking skills, giving students a chance to enrich their writing skills.
Grades 4–8 $11.95

For a complete listing of titles in this series, please visit our website at

http://www.prufrock.com

PRUFROCK PRESS INC.